# the little book of pocket mantras

## akasha moon, 2019

ISBN: 978-1-9995917-3-1

## About this Book and its Author

Akasha Moon was drawn to Hindu and Buddhist deities at an early age, learning to work consciously with their Mantras and Yantras following travels in India, China and Tibet particularly, where she found herself in respectful awe of their natural habitats, Temples, and the rituals performed therein.

She is deeply grateful to be living in an era in which meaningful experience may be derived from a diversity of cultural practices, and in which knowledge and techniques once reserved for the elite are finally available to all. She has embraced those that resonated with an open heart and the will to persist, exploring and practising ancient techniques in a cross-cultural, international context.

Because the results of these practices are so transformative and positive, this little book has emerged: a distilled collection of remedial mantras to lift the heart and inspire the reader and chanter. Ranging from easing physical pain, grief and depression, through protection and healing of self and others, to gaining and sustaining love, there is something in *The Little Book of Pocket Mantras* for everyone.

Akasha Moon (M.A. with Distinction) has worked as a Tarot-based psychic counsellor for over thirty years, and has written widely on Hindu, Egyptian and Greek deities, Magick, Witchcraft and the spiritual search in general. This book is the Eastern counterpart to her bestselling *Little Book of Pocket Spells,* published by Random House.

She is based in Glastonbury, England, where she lives with her husband and two very fine cats.

## Aum Gam Ganpataye Namah

All Hail Lord Ganesha!
Help keep us firm in spiritual integrity,
strengthen our resolve to complete what we
have started, and clear the way of obstacles.
Praises to universal source of wisdom,
knowledge, stamina, and the means to
perform practical good action!

## Introduction

A mantra is a focussed powerhouse of
word, vibration and image designed in
repetition to bring about a particular result.
*Manas* meaning mind, and *tra*, to protect and
defend, a mantra is thus a means of shielding
and liberating ones True Will from the
shackles of mental habit, physicality and even
Fate. Because Hinduism and Buddhism are so
fully cognisant of the efficacy of a mantra
reverently chanted, the most tried, effective
and time-honoured mantras belong to their
canons, and are largely in Sanskrit.

The mantras within these pages are presented phonetically, enabling those with no prior knowledge of Sanskrit to pronounce them in the relevant rhythm and as accurately as possible. Interpretive English translations are also provided in each section. The reader is encouraged to explore the resources listed at the back of this book for further illumination on context, meanings, and correct pronunciation.

While it is true that some believe a mantra only safe to use if received via a guru, this is impractical for most of us in the West. Besides, so many sacred mantras are now available via other sources that there seems no reason not to gather them into an easy-to-use format.

There is doubtless some validity in the accompanying belief of those who would rather keep mantras unsung by the uninitiated, that wrong pronunciation can bring bad results. Certainly, a difference of even an 'a' or 'h' can dramatically change a word and its import. Every effort has been made in this book to prevent such an incident. I would argue however that (a) Intent and focus and continual self-improvement can counteract this, and (b) Consider the habitual content of most people's minds: trivial concerns, fears, ego-ravings, sensationalist 'news', intrusive memories, gossip, food, sex, pleasure-seeking, and involuntary emotional loops, in the main. It seems inconceivable that any mantra, however badly chanted, could fail to be an improvement on this.

This book is intended to be a handy portable list of mantras, and the reader is of course encouraged to research further, for example learning about the Hindu and Buddhist deities concerned, inquiring into the basics of Sanskrit, or at least of Yoga (Patanjali is perhaps the best place to start), and listening to and memorising the mantras as chanted by Brahmins or others whose pronunciation, raga and rhythm is indubitably accurate. Please see the back of this book for a list of recommended resources.

We are deeply fortunate to be living at a unique time in which the canons, principles and spiritually refining techniques of many effective belief systems are open to any with the will to read, and of course, to research the world wide web. Religion and spirituality have never been so open for full assimilation, bringing together the wisdom of many experts in diverse paths, with one's personal experience. At last, pernicious divisions are breaking down and the Cosmic Creator being recognised as one source with many different aspects and names. It is my belief, too, that many Hindu and Buddhist souls are reincarnating in the West in order to discover their faiths anew, with a refreshed inspiration near-impossible to access when one is brought up in any faith, with its inevitable protocols and perfunctory rites. Here and now, numerous and diverse techniques for self-refinement and enlightenment, initiatory rites, philosophies and rituals are finally out in the open, facilitating greater understanding and faster evolution. Alongside this comes a set of powerful tools to engender spiritual growth and all other needs and desires. For aeons reserved for the privileged – be that by by caste, gender or wealth – the means for personal connection with the Divine is now becoming globally revealed, and thus enabling the civilian to elevate their consciousness exponentially.

It is said that in the current era, or *Kali Yuga*, the most effective form of meditation is mantric. Luckily for us – it is also the easiest! In addition, energetic wavelengths of physical being have altered dramatically over the past decades, and are continuing to accelerate, challenging consensus reality, speeding up 'time' as we know it, and occasionally playing the kind of quantum tricks which science too is beginning to recognise as not merely confined to Science Fiction. A flummoxing truth recently 'revealed' for example is that the atom itself is mostly empty – inner space is a palpable fact – yet how can this be? Our dull old paradigms are crumbling from 'solid fact' into the spaces between stardust, and every day the human species and all else in the cosmos is being revealed as part of the living mind of the Creative Source. Day by day the evolutionary ethers are refining and we are, perhaps paradoxically, growing closer to our origins.

So, how to bring that source of all happiness more fully into our lives, and how to access this *Ānanda*, this ultimately blissful state? Obviously that to which we attune our minds – what precisely we select from the cosmos to light up the screen of our individual consciousness, effects our emotional and spiritual states too, hence the now-popular adage: 'Where Thought goes, Energy flows'. The visual/emotional/intellectual mind is not *all* that we are, but it exists midway as it were between eternal Spirit, and the physical body and its current circumstances. It stands to reason that the thoughts we play and replay in our minds filter both up and down to effect the entirety of our lives, spiritual and physical. However – many of these thoughts, inclinations and preferences that we believe make up our character, our 'selves', are in fact imposters. Unwittingly we have absorbed the agendas, words and deeds of innumerable others both alive and long-dead, most notably sociologically (your place in society, your religion, your 'duties' as they pertain to the body you were born into) and emotionally (the early conditioning received, the situations that have hurt you or made you temporarily happy – and still do). These Pavlovian inputs, amongst many others, have programmed the way our brains worked, creating automatic psycho-spiritual responses to specific external and internal stimulae. Memory is a terrible perpetuator of this, responding willy-nilly to random connections, and often dragging our emotions with it, and fulfilling the 'karma' of the past – that is, perpetuating the motion of something formerly extant – by 'manifesting' via the mind in the present. In the Samadhi Pada of *The Yoga Sutras*, Patanjali refers to 'vrittis' in the 'chitti' – the disturbing mindwaves that ruin the state of calm Being and reflection. Mantra is the form of Yoga best equipped to dispel and negate all of these soul-undermining *vrittis*.

All it takes is practise and repetition to access and stimulate the original purity of soul and enthusiasm buried deep beneath the layers of meaningless connection. This can be done to an extent via 'affirmations' – the native-language positive thoughts popular in the West – but if the oft-repeated images, words, rhythms and intonations have been especially formulated by enlightened beings, are redolent of ancient ritual used to raise the consciousness, and if their very wavelength is a pure form of specifically-selected cosmic sustenance –  as is the case with Sanskrit mantras –  then surely all the better?! The words and sounds may seem challenging at first, but the practitioner will soon see how holding a sacred intent in conjunction with chanting these seed-sounds, speeds, sanctifies and amazingly embellishes all meditative efforts.

Pronunciation, rhythm and even pitch being key, in this book for beginners phonetic Sanskrit is featured, with punctuated rhythm where applicable. This is followed by a summary in English of import of the appeal. The mantras are divided into an A-Z of requirements, so that aid for specific purposes may be easily selected. Deceptive in their simplicity, we only need to press the internal 'Play' button on these mantras, sustain the intent through repetition, and the rest will program itself.

Mantras may be repeated either mentally, employing the 'Great Voice' of inner consciousness to fill the mind with its sound, or vocally: murmured or chanted aloud. It may be helpful to begin with the latter and work backwards to silence, so that the imagined sounds are as clear as if they were spoken – but it is your choice.

It is extremely helpful to avail yourself of the many fine recordings of mantras recited or sung by Buddhist monks and Hindu Brahmins, and others adept in Sanskrit and other mantric languages in order to cement the sounds, often unusual to the Western ear, in your memory-banks. See the end of this book for suggestions.

**Where and When?**

To each mantra is a particularly propitious time of the day, moon phase, planetary aspect, and date of the year.

However, all of the chants here-included will work wonderfully at dawn, midday and dusk especially, but also as and when desired. The main point is to be in a suitably enthusiastic state.

A quiet, conducive outside spot, or pleasant room is always preferable, but once a mantra has been memorised (or you're carrying this book!), you can of course employ it anywhere at any time. Public transport, lunch break at work – whenever your attention is free.

That said, mantras can also be played at the back of the mind while doing other things, though this is after they have been specifically and consciously activated.

Fasting, particularly from all consumption of meat, will always make a mantra or any spiritual practise more powerful.

## How to chant?

There are of course prescribed ways to chant mantras or to *jaap,* as they are part of Hindu and Buddhist orthodox practise. This is always with a clean body, usually facing East, in a certain posture or *asana*...you can get as strict as you wish about following these time-honoured techniques and rituals, which may be easily sourced online.

For our purposes, however, anywhere comfortable will do: straighten your back, focus on the point between the eyebrows, take a deep, cleansing breath; and launch!

## How many times do I repeat the Mantra, and do I need a Mala?

A mala (chain of 108 beads and one 'Guru bead', similar to a rosary, on which to count the repetitions) is a useful tool, but not essential. If you make mantric meditation into a serious practise, however, they are a great asset; and additionally, the specific materials of which they are made can help attune you to various different deities and wavelengths. A mala is especially helpful if you wish to follow a regular practise such as a forty-day regular chanting of 108 of a particular mantra, or many sets of 108.

The number of recommended repetitions is infinite. Obviously, the more you chant the mantra, the more you become it and adopt its qualities.

If you are very pressed for time, three repetitions is always better than doing nothing at all, as is as many as you can manage.

The main point is the quality and intensity of your focus.

The following mantras are presented first in traditional spelling (which, unlike English, is not fixed, and therefore varies slightly between regions), and then phonetically, the rhythm being implied within the spacing. The reader should therefore find these mantras immediately useable and practical. They are immensely powerful not just through their sense, but owing to to the vibrations created when these specific words and syllables are activated.

The approximate translations that accompany them are provided for mental anchoring rather than chanting purposes...but, as ever, the choice is yours. Do whatever gets you to that point of divine inspiration and contact!

For now – relax, connect with the Breath of the Divine – and transform your inner and outer lives!

# ANGER, QUELLING:

**Mantra:** *Aum Shante Prashante Sarva Krodha Upasha Mani Swaha*

**Pronunciation and Metre:**

> **Om Shanti**
> **Preh-Shanti**
>
> **Sar-vey Kro-doe**
> **Pash-a-mani Swa-ha**
>
> **Om Shanti**
> **Shanti**
> **Shanti-he**
> (x108, plus as required)

## Accompanying Meaning and Concepts:

All living beings are connected, and your individual-seeming pain and agitation effect everything negatively, not just yourself. How much more blissful then to contemplate peace and understanding! These principles create the sweet, all-benefitting salve of forgiveness.

Into my life I welcome Peace and Joy. May we each be freed from the painful shackles of resentment and wrath, and may Supreme Understanding reign always!

Aum Shanti, Shanti, Shanti...

# ANIMALS, RELATING TO, HELPING AND HEALING:

ॐ

**Mantra:** *Aum Pashupatayei Namaha*

## Pronunciation and Metre:

### Om Pasha-pat-eye-yay
### Nama-ha
(x108, plus as required)

## Accompanying Meaning and Concepts:

Hail Shiva Pashupati, Lord of the Animals! You who know the inner thoughts of each creature upon earth, their needs and desires! Please help me bring comfort, love and empathy to this beautiful animal (/all animals), as much a part of the sentient world as I am. Help me relate to the nature of things, the primal pulse and pull of instinct, the emotional response that comes from living as this particular creature, that we may live in harmony on earth, devoid of species-arrogance and cruelty.

Salutations to the living Creator, whose consciousness exists in all things! Salutations to all the beautiful animals of the earth and beyond!

ॐ

# ATHLETIC STAMINA AND PROWESS

**Mantra: *Aum Han Hanumate Namo Namah, Shri Hanumate Namo Namah, Jai Jai Hanumate Namo Namah, Shri Ram Dutaay Namo Namah***

## Pronunciation and Metre:

**Om Han-Hanumat-ay, Namo Nama-ha
Shree Hanumat-ay, Namo Nama-ha
Jay-Jay Hanumat-ay, Namo Nama-ha
Shree Ram Duta-yay, Namo Nama-ha**

(Repeat with a speed and jaunty rhythm that best reflects the spirit of your aspiration/potential feat, x108 +)

## Accompanying Meaning and Concepts:

Envisage yourself absorbing the formidable qualities of this simian hero of the Ramayana, esteemed Lord Hanuman: the swiftest, most steadfast and agile of Lord Rama's disciples, armoured against enemies and ever-steadfast in intent. See yourself succeeding in your sport or activity of choice, and growing ever-stronger as you chant, each syllable pumping the cells of your body with extra energy and the will to succeed.

Salutations, Lord Hanuman, I praise your superhuman stamina and monkey agility! Through constant repetition of your mantra, I by your grace imbue myself with similar qualities.

Victory unto you; and on the physical planes, may I reflect your success!

# BEAUTY/PHYSICAL ATTRACTION

**Mantra:** *Aum Namo Bhagwate Rukmini Vallabhaaye Swaha*

**Pronunciation and Metre:**

**Om Namo Bhaga-vat-e**
**Ruk-mini**
**Valla-beye-ya**
**Swa-ha**
(x108, plus as required)

## Accompanying Meaning and Concepts:

Hail Rukmini, enchanting consort of the all-attractive Lord Krishna! I bow to thee and surrender to ineffable Divine Love! Kindly endow me with your quiet confidence, grace, strength, and indubitable beauty; may I too be attractive of both body and soul, full of the qualities that provoke and sustain desire in the reciprocative partner of my choice.

Beauty and love to all: So Mote It Be!

# CONTENTMENT

**Mantra:** *Hari Aum Tat Sat*

**Pronunciation and Metre:**

> **Hari Om, Tat Sat**
> **Hari Om, Tat Sat**
> **Hari Om**
> **Hari Om**
> **Hari Om, Tat Sat**

## Accompanying Meaning and Concepts:

> Aum is All and All is Aum.
> That is Everything.
>
> Contemplate.

# COMMUNICATION, Increased powers of

**Mantra:** *Haam, Vak, Aum Braam Breem Braun, Sah Buddhaya namah*

**Pronunciation and Meter:**

**Haam**
**Vak**
**Aum Braam**
**Bree-m Braun**
**Sah Budd-haya**
**Nama-ha**
(as required)

## Accompanying Meaning and Concepts:

With these intonations, I open my mind and throat for better, more spontaneous and precise communications. By this repetition I declare my will to hone and finesse my verbal fluency and confidence.

May I flow in the rhythm and zone of perfected intent and intelligence! Powers of Mercury, I invoke you! May I not stumble on self-doubt, but know that with the correct cosmic guidance to which I now appeal, all is for a purpose, and is as it should be.

May every sound I utter be guided by Vak, and by divine Wisdom!

# CONFIDENCE (AGAINST ENMITY)
## See also PROTECTION

**Mantra:** *Aum Graam Greem Graum Sauh Gurave Namaha*

**Pronunciation and Meter:**
> **Om Gram Greem Graum**
> **Sah Guru-vey**
> **Nama-ha**
> (x108)

## Accompanying Meaning and Concepts:

Visualising light blue light with a golden inner glow, inwardly salute the vast powers of Jupiter. Feel its qualities imbuing you as you chant.

O planetary force and celestial mentor, invest in me your powers of wisdom, nurturing expansion, confidence, and benign victory. May I emanate steady gravitas and yet joy, may I inspire admiration even in my enemies, and may the steadfast qualities of honour and wisdom ever abide within me!

I give praise to the quiet strength luminaries who have gone before, and wish to cut my own character in a similarly fine cloth.

May my courage increase with every repetition of this mantra!

# CREATIVITY (/Originality)

**Mantra:** *Aum Hreem Shreem Saraswatyai Namah*

**Pronunciation and Metre:**

**Om Hreem Shreem
Saras-wat-eye-ay
Nama-ha**
(x108, plus as required)

## Meaning and Concepts:

Oh Sarasvati, beauteous Goddess of knowledge, music and the Arts, I greet you! Kindly bless me with your radiant qualities of free-flowing energy, understanding, and original thought. May thesis and antithesis meet in me as spectacular synthesis, by the power of your mantra and your sacred name that I here repeat!

# DEPRESSION, LESSENING & HEALING; FACILITATING RECOVERY

**Mantra:** *Tataya Aum, Bekandze, Bekandze, Maha Bekandze, Radza Samudgate Soha*

**Pronunciation and Metre:**

> **Tat-ay-a Om**
> **Bek-and-zee**
> **Bek-and-zee**
> **Ma-ha Bek-and-zee**
> **Radza Sum-ud-gat-ay**
> **So-ha**

(x108, plus as required)

## Accompanying Meaning and Concepts:

As you recite this mantra of the Medicine Buddha, gentle relief will flood into your energy centres like soft morning light.

May all ailments be lifted from me (/the subject of this meditation) and from all other beings! May that which blights us and shadows our lives be recognised as a necessary lesson, learned – and dismissed!

# EGO, SHEDDING (Brings Personal Relief and Cosmic Perspective to any Situation)

ॐ

**Mantra:** *Aum Hreem Namay Shivaya*

**Pronunciation and Metre:**

**Om Hreem, Namah Shiv-eye-yah**

(x108, plus as required)

**Accompanying Meaning and Concepts:**

As you repeat Shiva's sacred mantra, envisage the sound 'Hreem' slicing through your attachments to the objects and emotions you define as 'you', knowing that these things bear no meaning on the other side of the Veil, in the true world of Eternal Spirit.

All Hail Shiva, Supreme Yogi and Lord of Transcendence of the Physical! As I repeat your name, I surrender to the Universe, replacing personal concerns with joyous detachment. May hardship be felt as meaningful penance and discipline, an outer symbol of inner initiation, and embracing all that comes my way, and all that Is, may I grow ever closer to the Divine.

Knowing that in this incalculable cosmos I am but a mote, a fleeting cluster of unregulated feelings, thoughts and random connections, may I be invested with the wisdom to treat all circumstances as living *leelas*, plays of the Divine, and thus treat them with the levity they deserve. May I be entertained rather than pained by the mini-dramas of this little life.

I understand that all other living creatures are my equals, and I pledge to treat them as such.

May every situation I encounter be met with equal fervour for enlightenment, and may the needful sense of self-preservation and motivation always be balanced with the knowledge of this body's ultimate insignificance.

Aum Namah Shiva!

# EXAMS, PASSING

**Mantra:** *Aum Saumya Sarasvatei Namah*

**Pronunciation and Metre:**

## Om Saum-a Sarasvati-yay Nama-ha

(x108, plus as required)

**Accompanying Meaning and Concepts:**

Oh great Goddess Saraswati, divine epitome of culture, wisdom and success in studies, please bless me as I face these exams. As I chant these sacred syllables I feel myself invested with calmness, excellent memory, and presence of mind. May I use the skills and qualifications thus acquired for the greater good of All.

## FERTILITY (physical)

**Mantra:** *Aum Shree Kamakhya Namah*

**Pronunciation and Metre:**

**Om Shri**
**Kama-Khya-yay**
**Nama-ha**
(x108 plus as required)

## Accompanying Meaning and Concepts:

To be repeated by either, or preferably both of the potential parents. Can also be listened to while lovemaking. Fasting, especially from all consumption of meat, will always make a mantra more powerful.

Oh Khamakhya, Goddess of desire and making of form through Love, may Shiva and Shakti unite within our bodies to create and bring forth healthy new life! May our joy in life and will to bring more light of love to earth prevail, and may our resulting progeny be strong in mind, body and spirit!

## FORGIVENESS (Of Others, and Self)

ॐ

**Mantra: *Aum Kshamaye Namah***

**Pronunciation and Metre:**

**Aum
Kshamay-ae
Nama-ha**
(x108, plus as required)

## Accompanying Meaning and Concepts:

This mini-mantra is derived from a more complex prayer begging forgiveness for blunders and oversights unwillingly made.

Ultimately, malice springs from misery and ignorance, and thus should be pitied rather than exacerbated with vengeful thoughts.

*Forgiveness is a gift you give yourself.* Contrary to how it may feel, it does not exonerate the hurtful party; rather, it exemplifies a wider world-view in which we accept that despite some Free Will, we are all actors in a theatre of Duality, subject to synapse-connections, nerve-impulses and gut reactions almost – though not entirely – beyond our control.

Often, negative-seeming scenarios are enacted in order to test and develop our own mettle. The individual channels for these encounters 'know not what they do'; they are helpless against the Greater Plan, and most often blinkered to it. To assimilate this can bring great relief from anger and regret.

Aum: may we rise above petty self-concerns and ego-hurts, and contemplate with compassionate awareness the million circumstances hidden from our sight!

# HEALING (Emotional)

**Mantra:** *Ramadasa Sa So Say Hung*

**Pronunciation and Metre:**

**Raa Ma Da Sae
Sa Say So Hung**

(Softly, as required)

## Accompanying Meanings and Concepts:

O Ra the Sun, Ma the Moon, Da the Earth and Sa the Light and Love eternal, attune me to your healing wavelengths! Let any dissonances in my Being be dissolved in your Cosmic Harmonies!

May the waves of this mantra as I repeat it flow across and through these bodies, smoothing and soothing all rough edges, healing the cracks and fissures in body and soul, and may I absorb and emanate comfort, love and peace as I go forth into this small slice of reality that I know as 'the world'.

# HEALING (Physical)

**Mantra:** *Aum Tum Tulasaye Namah*

**Pronunciation and Metre:**

**Om Tum**
**Tula-sai-ye**
**Nama-ha**
(x108, plus as required)

## Accompanying Meaning and Concepts:

Oh sweet, protective spirit of the Divine, made manifest here on earth in the plant we know as Tulsi or Basil, may this body be filled with your fragrant comfort and revitalising properties!

May each good cell be flushed with health like your greenest leaves, and disease and discomfort be purified and dispelled!

AUM...

# HEALING (Surgical/Medical Intervention)

ॐ

**Mantra:** *Aum Gam Ganapataye Namaha*

**Pronunciation and Metre:**

**Om Gam
Ganap-atay-yay
Nama-ha**

(x108, plus as required, on as many days as possible prior to and during procedure)

## Accompanying Meaning and Concepts:

Sweet-tempered Ganesh, Lord of Surgeons, Doctors and Medical care, please bless this operation with the precision, cleanliness, and all the propitious circumstances it requires to succeed!

# INSPIRATION

**Mantra: *Har Har Mukunday***

**Pronunciation and Metre:**

> **Har Har Mukun-day**
> **Har Har Mukun-day**
> **Har Har Mukun-day**

(as much as feels effectively uplifting)

**Accompanying Meaning and Concepts:**

All hail great Liberator from the illusion of entrapment!

Although our beguiling prisons of flesh often make us ignore or forget the bigger picture, we are each actually Spirits in the material world, able at any time – with focus and persistence – to go within and access the Divine Source of all Creation. For, just as we and all civilisations and all creatures and plants and elements have been bred by the Earth, and just as the earth and suns and stars and planets have been borne of the Creative Intelligence, so too do we have entire Universes within us, waiting to be Real-ized and made palpable...

Great Liberator, I beseech you to bring a suitable bolt of your Cosmic Inspiration my way!

ॐ

# INTERVIEW – Acing, and JOB/PROMOTION – Attaining

ॐ

**Mantra:** *Aum Geem Goom Ganapate Namah Swaha*

**Pronunciation and Metre:**

**Om Geem Goom
Gana-pat-ay
Namah
Swa-ha**
(x108, and as needed)

## Accompanying Meaning and Concepts:

Envisage a golden glow gathering around you as you recite this mantra.

O Future Employer, see how I am substantial and knowing like the elephant, capable of carrying great burdens effortlessly: what a transformative addition I will make to your enterprise! May the beneficent circumstances and jovial properties of expansion innate to the great God Ganesha bless me as I make this bid for regular work and wage. See how I am the adept problem-solver and precise worker whom you seek, who will help take your endeavours to the next level!

Aum, and thank you, mighty Ganesha!

ॐ

# INTRUSIVE THOUGHTS – COMBATTING

**Mantra:** *Hare Krishna Hare Krishna, Krishna Krishna Hare Hare, Hare Rama Hare Rama, Rama Rama Hare Hare*

**Pronunciation and Metre:**

> **Haar-ay Krishna Haar-ay Krishna**
> **Krishna Krishna Haar-ay Haar-ay**
> **Haar-ay Rama Haar-ay Rama**
> **Rama Rama Haar-ay Haar-ay**

**Accompanying Meaning and Concepts:**

Intrusive thoughts emanate primarily from trauma, insecurity, and any concomitant unprocessed anger. This simple and popular mantra makes an excellent replacement for destructive brain-loops, disrupting their habitual power and filling one's entire Being with spiritual aspiration and love of the Divine. Merely thinking it steps us up a level, bringing one closer to the ultimate salve, the all-pervading godhead in whichever expression you prefer to conceive of it.

The Krishna form of God is all-loving, playful, gentle, childlike and beautiful; and the music of his flute makes very short thrift of melancholic or disruptive influences upon the divine *leela*, the play of Cosmic Melodrama that is our daily lives.

Corrupt forces cannot withstand the power of this Agape, this great Love.

May dark thoughts scatter, and joy, levity of heart and adoration of the all-pervasive Divine, ever prevail!

# JUSTICE – (Receiving Fair Outcomes)

ॐ

**Mantra:** *Aum Kreem Mahakaliye Namah*

**Pronunciation and Metre:**

### Aum Kreem
### Maha-Kali-Kay-ai
### Nama-ha

(x1008 and as needed)

## Accompanying Meaning and Concepts:

With each repetition of this powerful mantra, envisage the protective electric blue light of Kali surrounding and protecting you, while your enemies are symbolically slain for their injustices. Your own purity of Soul and Will to see a fair outcome will provide the propulsion to set this balancing process into action.

Aum, Great Goddess Kali, who beheads the Ego and terminates all selfish desires; whose roots and origin are Love and Fairness for All; I appeal to you now, confident under your aegis that Divine Justice will always prevail!

O sacred warrior-goddess who protects the weak and defiled, whose righteous anger causes the greatest of men and demons to quake in humility: be by my side in this, my battle for Justice, I beseech you!

ॐ

## LOVE – (Cosmic/Divine: for confidence, inspiration and protection)

ॐ

**Mantra:** *Radhe Krishna Radhe Krishna Krishna Krishna Radhe Radhe, Radhe Sham, Radhe Sham, Sham Sham Radhe Radhe*

**Pronunciation and Metre:**

**Rha-day Krishna Rha-day Krishna
Krishna Krishna Rha-day Rha-day
Rha-day Shaam Rha-day Shaam
Shaam Shaam Rha-day Rha-day**
(as required)

**Accompanying Meaning and Concepts:**

Contemplating the celestial beauty of the endless source of Cosmic Love, the Shiva-Shakti dynamic personified by Krishna and his exquisite consort Radha, we offer kindness and joy to all beings upon Earth! We understand that we can love Krishna (or our chosen divinity) with all our hearts, trusting completely, and fearing no pain such as will always arise from human desire.

For, engaged in chanting Your name and contemplating You, we need no other. You are the essence of all Joy, Repletion, Growth and Understanding.

God is Love: and Love is, indeed, all that we need.

Hare Krishna!

Constant chanting of Krishna mantras, either aloud or in your head, will refine your sensibilities, increase your artistic skills, and elevate you on all levels.

# LOVE – (Friendship: attracting, mending and sustaining)

ॐ

**Mantra:** *Aum Vijaya Ganapate Namaha*

## Pronunciation and Metre:

**Om Vee-jay-a
Gana-pat-eye-ay
Nama-ha**
(x108 and as feels good)

## Accompanying Concepts and Meanings:

As you chant this mantra, visualise your aura emanating orange-yellow light, and expanding.

AUM, Lord Ganesh who is victorious over all obstacles, I greet thee! Kindly bless me with strong and honourable allies, and keep clear the channels between me, my current companions and those good folk who may yet become my friends, so that all communications between us are blessed by your great benevolence, and all situations are tempered by your wisdom and humour.

# LOVE – (Marital: for Nurturing, Happiness and Fidelity)

**Mantra: *Aum Laxmi Narayana Namaha***

## Pronunciation and Metre:

**Om Lax-mi
Naray-ana-ya
Nama-ha**
(x108 plus)

## Accompanying Meaning and Concepts:

Greetings to the Goddess of good fortune, Laxmi, and her loving consort Lord Narayana! May my repetitions of this ancient and powerful mantra endow my marriage with the same blessings that You share, and may You shower us with love and happiness as golden and eternal as Your own!

## LOVE – (Self: Feeling a Worthy part of the Cosmos, Knowing You are Part of God)

ॐ

**Mantra: *Aum Shivoham***

**Pronunciation and Metre:**

### Om Shiv-o-ham

(as required)


**Accompanying Meaning and Concepts:**


As I contemplate the divinely complex simplicity of Creation, I celebrate the fact that I am a living microcosm of the powers of Creation, Preservation and Destruction. We are each made of the matter of the Cosmos. We are part of Everything that ever Was, and Ever Shall Be.

AUM – Shiva!  Aum – everything is Shiva (/God)! Aum – I too am Shiva(/God)!
O great Lord of Yogis, perfect our imperfections and shatter our illusions! So that, with no need to strain for thought and action – simply by Being – we may exist in the understanding that I am, You are; we All are – Eternal Spirit.

ॐ

## LOVE – (Sexual: to enhance within an established relationship)
## (See also: Sexual Energy)

ॐ

**Mantra: *Aum Kleem Kamakhaye Namah***

**Pronunciation and Metre:**

**Om Kleem
Kama-Khay-ey
Nama-ha**
(x108 and as needed)

**Accompanying Meaning and Concepts:**

Imagine soft rose-coloured light enveloping you as you chant this sacred mantra, imbuing you with beauty on all levels. Feel it surrounding also the partner of your choice.

O Kamakhaye, great Goddess of Love and Attraction, I greet Thee! Bless, I beseech You, the relationship for which I chant, with greater sexual energy and interaction.

May its every intimacy be enhanced by your boundless spiritual beauty!

Aum!

ॐ

## MONEY – Attracting

ॐ

**Mantra:** *Aum Shri Mahalaxmi Namah*

**Pronunciation and Metre:**

**Om**
**Shree**
**Maha-Lax-mi**
**Namah-ha**
(Every day as much as possible)

## Accompanying Meanings and Concepts:

Just as the Lotus flower floats on the lake, may I(/we) float on the Waters of Life, effortlessly carried by the beneficence of the Universe! As the petals of the Lotus are perfect, so too may my body and other physical circumstances flourish without tarnish, no matter what the background and circumstances.

May my skin glow with health and wealth, as if a thousand ghee lamps of the goddess Laxmi were burning softly in my Soul.

Beauty, Love, and good Fortune be mine, that I might spread my wealth and joy on to others, just as the hands of the great Goddess herself are always open and shedding coins, even as She receives our humble offerings.

Aum Shri Mahalaxmi Namah!

ॐ

## NIGHTMARES – Banishing

ॐ

**Mantra: *Aum Dum Durgaye Namah***

## Pronunciation and Metre:

**Om**
**Dum Durgay-yay**
**Nama-ha**
(x 108 before you go to bed, and as many
times as needed as you drift off)

## Accompanying Meaning and Concepts:

As you chant this ancient, sacred and
protective formula, see how the darkness
dispels itself, helplessly evaporating as you
repeat the formidable invocation of Ma Durga.

May the Protection of the fiercest Mother
surround this, Her sleeping child! See how Her
bladed hands whirl with fighting fury against
any ghost, ghoul or living thing that would
hunt you in your sleep or waking life! No
demon or dark thing dares to show its face,
and all of ill intent are deterred by Her
terrifying three-eyed stare. With Her psychic
vision She knows every trick in the book, so
there can be no nasty surprises, no hidden evil
eye, not a trace remaining of anything malign!

Now you may sleep as softly as any babe cradled in the infinite love of the Divine Mother.

*Tatasthu*!

So Mote It be!

# PAIN-QUELLING (Physical and Emotional)

ॐ

**Mantra: *Aum Hum Hanumate Rudratmakaye Hum Phat***

## Pronunciation and Metre:

**Om Hum
Hanu-mat-ay
Rudra-ma-kay-eh
Hum
Phat**
(as required)

## Accompanying Meaning and Concepts:

Most of us know physical pain – along with anger and grief – to be among the most spiritually distracting phenomenon possible. It may all be ultimately sublimating, and wisdom may dictate that it's bound to be for some higher reason in the longer term; but how to find relief from this cruel cul-de-sac of the senses?

The Cosmic Intelligence has divided itself into many helpful Avatars; and one who can help assuage and heal physical pain is Hanuman, the monkey god and Ayurvedic expert who quite literally moved mountains to help heal Lord Rama in that famous epic, *The Ramayana*.

May this mantra sooth with its repetitive soothing syllables, and put pain in its rightful place – PHAT! – gone!

ॐ

## PEACE ON EARTH, PLEASE

ॐ

**Mantra: *Aum Shanti, Shanti, Shanti***

**Pronunciation and Metre:**

### Om Shanti,
### Shanti,
### Shanti-he
(softly, for as long as wished)

## Accompanying Meaning and Concepts:

'It is so simple to be happy, but so difficult to be simple', as Paramahansa Yogananda deftly summarised in his spiritual classic *Autobiography of a Yogi*. AUM is the essence of meaningful simplicity. This multi-faceted syllable on its own, levels all with its pervasive eternal vibration that creates, sustains, destroys and recycles life itself.

Complete it with the shushing ancient sibilants of the Shanti mantra, and let Peace, Compassion and Understanding prevail.

Aum Shanti, Shanti, Shanti-he...

ॐ

# PROTECTION (Physical)

ॐ

**Mantra:** *Aum Namo Bhagavataye Vasudevaya*

**Pronunciation and Metre:**

## Om Namo
## Bhagavat-ay
## Vasu-deva-eye-ya

(x108)

## Accompanying Meaning and Concepts:

If you are under physical threat, take appropriate measures on the physical plane to back up this powerful mantra for courage, invisibility, and good luck under duress.

As you chant and repeat the sacred syllables, envisage yourself growing ever stronger and more unassailable. In addition to developing and enhancing these qualities, this mantra of the great Preserver Vishnu will help keep your environment clear of encroachers and anyone of harmful intent.

# PROTECTION (Psychic)

ॐ

**Mantra:** *Aum Namo Hanumate Rudravatarya, Parayantra Mantra Tantra, Tataka Nashakaya, Sri Rama Duraye Swaha*

## Pronunciation and Metre:

Om Namo Hanu-ma-tay
Rudr-ava-tar-eye-a
Para-Yantra
Mantra
Tantra
Tat-a-ka Nashak-eye-a
Sri Rama
Dutay-eh
Swa-ha

(x108)

## Accompanying Meaning and Concepts:

All hail Hanuman, all hail Lord Ram: please revitalise and keep safe my pranic energy!

I repeat these magickal mantric verses for strength, stability, and protection against all enmity and assault, knowing that all negativity is decimated as it strikes the Aura that You have thus Blessed.

# PROTECTION (Of Self/Anything or Anyone, including Child or Animal)

**Mantra: *AUM***

**Pronunciation and Metre:**

**AAAAAAUUUUUUMMMM**
**AAAAAAUUUUUUMMMM**
**AAAAAAUUUUUUMMMM**
(Ad Infinitum!)


## Accompanying Meaning and Concepts:

Of course the AUM is incorporated into all mantras – it is the spine around which the other sounds arrange themselves – but chanting it on its own is one of the most powerful practises possible. It has infinite qualities of enlightenment, and can be used protectively to great effect.

Visualise the beloved person, pet or even property surrounded by and glowing with the desired quality, and send your heartfelt love and strength into the protective shield of crackling electric blue light as you loose yourself in repetition of this, the most fundamental and sacred of sounds.

AUM...

## PSYCHIC POWERS, Attaining

ॐ

**Mantra:** *Om Sadashivaye Trinetra Jagritaya Purnatvam Drudhryam Rudraye Namah*

**Pronunciation and Metre:**

**Om
Sadha Shiv-eye-yay
Tree-nate-rah Jag-ra-tar-yay
Pur-nat-wa
Drush-am
Rudr-ah-yay
Nama-ha**
(x108, as much as possible)

## Accompanying Meaning and Concepts:

As you chant or mentally repeat this mantra, focus on the space between your eyebrows and on 'seeing' through it. Envisage all distractions reduced to ashes as you blast through them with your focus and determination.

May my Third Eye, like that of Lord Shiva, be ever-open! May I have the self-discipline required to access and wisely handle all psychic powers. I intuit how even suffering can become a *siddhi*, a bonus power, and thus willingly do I accept and assimilate all that the Universe has to show me.

The more you repeat and practise any of the mantras in this book, the more psycho-spiritually refined and powerful you will become. This one will certainly increase your everyday psychic abilities.

# PURITY/SPIRITUAL INTEGRITY

ॐ

**Mantra: *Aum Mani Padme Hum***

**Pronunciation and Metre:**

> **Om Mani Padme Hum**
> (softly, and as required)

## Accompanying Meanings and Concepts:

This beautiful mantra, ubiquitous throughout Tibet, India and Nepal, is famous for its simplicity and efficacy.

O Divine Buddha of Compassion, also known as Avalokisteshvara: as I admire the perfection of the gem of your wisdom at the heart of the cosmic lotus, and as I repeat this gentle mantra, please align All that I Am with the principles of Love, Kindness, Wisdom, Patience and Purity of Intent.

May my mind, soul and body be strong pure.

Blessings to All upon earth.

Amen and Aum!

ॐ

# SECURITY, Sense of
## (Also acts as Spiritual Guidance, and Protection)

ॐ

**Mantra:** *Aum Bhur Bhuva Swaha, Tat Sevitur Vareynyum, Bhargo Devaysa Dimahi, Dhyo Yona Prochodhyat*

**Pronunciation and Metre:**

> **Om Bhuur Boo-va Swah-ha**
> **Tat Sevi-tur Ver-eyn-yum**
> **Bhargo Dev-ysa Dhi-mah-hi**
> **Dhiyo Yonaf Pra-cho-die-at**

(x108 daily, preferably at dawn, and as required)

## Accompanying Meaning and Concepts:

The Gayatri Mantra is an entity in Herself, a five-faced Goddess by whose guidance we may perceive the brilliance of the all-encompassing Spiritual Sun. By repeating this mantra, we thank and praise the Creative Source, worshipped here as the Solar Logos, for the many blessings of the world, affirming our rightful place as part of the great Creation, and requesting greater insight, intelligence, and all good properties to come forth into our conscious lives.

This elevating mantra is a cornerstone of Hinduism and a vast blessing to humanity, its every syllable carrying our Souls closer and closer to Divine Truth.

It therefore brings great happiness, health, cosmic blessings, protection on all levels, and wisdom to those who avail themselves of it on a regular basis.

This mantra is one of the ultimate Cosmic Armours!

## SEXUAL ENERGY (See also Love, sexual)

**Mantra: *Lam Vam, Sam Sam Sam, Bam Bham Mam, Yam Ram Lam***

**Pronunciation and Metre:**

**Lam Vam
Sam Sham Scham
Bam Bham
Mam Yam
Ram Lam**
(deeply and slowly, as required)

These *bijas* (seed-sounds) may be vibrated and repeated while visualising the Chakra at the root of the spine (Lam) and Sacral Chakra (Vam) respectively. The other sounds relate to the petals of these Lotus-Chakras.

Over thousands of years, Rishis and Yogis have perfected the power of sound as an activating and elevating Cosmic Energy: these simple syllables are deeply effective; so use them gradually, and with care.

## SLEEP – Attaining/Improving

**Mantra:** *Aum Aum Hun Hun Aum, Aum Aum Hum Hum Aum*

**Pronunciation and Metre:**

### Om Om Hun Hun Aum
### Om Om Hum Hum Aum

(softly and slowly, as required)

### Accompanying Meaning and Concepts:

Repeat this soothing astral *mala,* or rosary of seed-sounds, aloud a few times before bed, and then in your head as you try to drift off. Don't forget to separate the Huns from the Hums...

# SPIRITUALITY – Increasing
## (for Spiritual Courage, Insight, Stamina, Protection...)

ॐ

**Mantra:** *Aum Aim Hreem Kleem, Chamundaye Vicche*

**Pronunciation and Metre:**

> **Om Eye-m Hreem Kleem**
> **Cham-unday-eh Vee-chi**
> (x108)

## Accompanying Meaning and Concepts:

May the powers of Saraswati, Laxmi and Kali (here combined in *Durga Chamunda*) act as a shield against ignorance, lethargy, and negative wavelengths!

May I be fierce against my own ego-trivia, and strong in protecting that which is truly important as I traverse this, the Maya-Matrix of distraction and illusion.

## STRENGTH (Physical, and in Challenging Situations in which You are Justified)

ॐ

**Mantra:** *Shri Ram Jai Ram, Jai Jai Ram*

**Pronunciation and Metre:**

**Shree Raam**
**Jay Raam**
**Jay Jay Raam**
(repeat as required)

### Accompanying Meaning and Concepts:

As you chant these enlivening syllables, focus on the principles of utmost integrity; on facing all battles with valour, in the knowledge that you serve the principles of Good. Feel the sounds surrounding you like gleaming armour.

I am true unto Myself and to those whom I most respect. Like the intrepid Lord Hanuman, may I serve and fight selflessly for higher principles, here symbolised by Lord Rama as Guru or Higher Self, whilst cleverly protecting myself from attacks and negativity of any sort.
I am protected by my own rectitude, and stalwart in my carefully-formulated decisions. Therefore, victory be unto the Best of Me.
*Tatastu*, and AUM!

ॐ

## STRENGTH (Of Spirit/Resolve)

ॐ

**Mantra: *Hare Aum Nama Shivaye***

**Pronunciation and Metre:**

**Hari Om
Namah Shiv-eye-yay**
(x108 plus)

## Accompanying Meaning and Concepts:

Absorbing the qualities of this sacred chant as
I repeat it, may I be ever-perceptive of those
who would deter me from my chosen path;
may I be stalwart in my choices; may I have
the strength of abnegation that Lord Shiva in
his ascetic aspect so beautifully exemplifies,
going ever inward to find reserves of
willpower, courage and worthy aspiration.

May I not be bedazzled by the baubles of
material life and society, but persist even
against all odds, eternally supplied with
fortitude physical, mental and – above all –
Spiritual!

## STUDY – Enhancing

**Mantra:** *Aum Aim Hreem Shreem,*
*Vagdevyai Sarasvatei Namah*

**Pronunciation and Metre:**

**Om**
**I'm**
**Hreem**
**Shreem**
**Vaag-devi-eye**
**Saras-wat-ee-eye**
**Nama-ha**

**Accompanying Meaning and Concepts:**

Breathing deeply and mentally imbibing the pure ethers of the divine realms, chant these sacred seed-sounds and syllables of praise to Saraswati, Goddess of Knowledge and Matron of students.

With the blessing of these ancient powers, I hone my mind and skills of communication to a fine point of precision. May Divine Knowledge, Comprehension, and Inspiration accompany my studies!

## THIRD EYE STIMULATION

**Mantra: *Aum Hrim Namah Shivaye***

**Pronunciation and Metre:**

### Om Hrim Namah Sheev-eye-a

(vigorously, x108+)


**Accompanying Meaning and Concepts:**

As you chant these sacred syllables of Shiva, Lord of Yogis, feel them pressing at the inside of your head just between the eyebrows, and emerging as brilliant blue light that illuminates everything around, before, and even behind you. You may like to accompany this practise with a physical bindi or dot between the eyes, preferably of sandalwood, turmeric, or *kumkum* if you can get or make it. Rosewater or fresh spring water will also work well to help stimulate the Ajna Chakra on which you focus as you chant.

   With regular practise, expect petty concerns to drop away and priorities to change, possibly dramatically: for this mantra will dramatically expand your perspective on reality...

   *Tatastu*, and AUM!

# FURTHER READING AND RESEARCH

## Books:

Patanjali – The Yoga Sutras (many versions available)

Yogananda, Paramahansa – *Autobiography of a Yogi* (published by the Self-Realization Fellowship)

## Websites and online Resources:

***Please note that none of the following is in any way connected with this book or its author:***

www.ananda.org

www.mysticalbee.com

www.yogajournal.com

Arsha Bodha Center (YouTube)

Hindu Academy (YouTube)

Gaiea Sanskrit (YouTube)

Kundalini Yogini (YouTube)

Rajsri Soul (YouTube)

The Sanskrit Channel (YouTube)

Sanskrit Mantras (YouTube)

**See also:**

**www.kalatrobe.com**, where you can find links to a selection of superb online mantras

### Music:

Lakshmy Ratheesh & Radhika Venugopal

Deva Premal & Miten

Saindhavi

Uma Mohan

Varsha Dwidevi

## A Few Points to Ponder

One life contains many personae: we are not the same character at seventy as we were at thirty, or three years old. Likewise does creation encapsulate numerous personae, all ultimately of the same source, and fundamentally united, but at differing stages of progress.

We are all Spirit on a material journey.

Spirit is One – 'Self' is merely consciousness fragmented.

Physical matter is a temporary illusion of Ultimate Reality.

To help another is to help your Self – this is sheer logic, not spiritual materialism – likewise; hurt another, and you hurt us All.

Imagination, combined with the discernment of true integrity, is the vehicle of many truths and evolutionary principles.

Purity of Heart and Intent is the absolute best we can ask of ourselves and others.

To each, their own Path; that is, their own current Truth and Belief.

Mutual Respect is *the* most powerful tool for intellectual and spiritual growth.

A-U-M

Printed in Great Britain
by Amazon

23519952R00042